A Publication of the AAHE Forum on Faculty Roles & Rewards

DEPARTMENTAL ASSESSMENT

How Some Campuses Are Effectively Evaluating the Collective Work of Faculty

by JON F. WERGIN *and* JUDI N. SWINGEN

Companion volume to
The Collaborative Department: How Five Campuses Are Inching Toward Cultures of Collective Responsibility

American Association for Higher Education

The research reported in this paper

was supported by a grant from

The Pew Charitable Trusts.

Views expressed here are

those of the authors.

■

DEPARTMENTAL ASSESSMENT: How Some Campuses Are Effectively Evaluating the Collective
Work of Faculty
by Jon F. Wergin and Judi N. Swingen

Additional copies of this publication or Jon Wergin's *The Collaborative Department: How Five Campuses Are
Inching Toward Cultures of Collective Responsibility* (1994) are available from:

    AMERICAN ASSOCIATION FOR HIGHER EDUCATION

    One Dupont Circle, Suite 360, Washington, DC 20036-1110

    Ph 202/293-6440, Fax 202/293-0073

    www.aahe.org/catalog

AAHE Item #FR0003   ISBN 1-56377-049-0

ABOUT THE AUTHORS

Jon F. Wergin has served as senior scholar at AAHE for its New Pathways Project and has consulted widely on topics related to faculty and program assessment. He is professor of educational studies at Virginia Commonwealth University.

Judi N. Swingen received her Ph.D. in education from Virginia Commonwealth University in 1999, and currently serves as a research associate at its Graduate School.

Contents

Methods and Procedures 5

Campus Evaluation Practices 6
    Program review 6
    Outcomes assessment 7
    Specialized accreditation 8
    Financial accounting initiatives 9
    Internal quality assurance 10

Components of Effective Evaluation
at the Departmental Level 12
    Organizational and Cultural Setting 12
        A leadership of engagement 12
        Engaged departments 13
        A culture of evidence 14
        A culture of peer collaboration and peer review 14
        A respect for differences 15
        Evaluation with consequence 15
    Evaluation Policies and Practices 15
        A clear purpose that fits the culture and mission of the institution 16
        "Spirit of inquiry" by the central administration 16
        Tangible administrative follow-through 17
    Evaluation Standards, Criteria, and Measures 17

Recommendations for Evaluation Practice 21
    Be proactive in discussions of "quality" 21
    Decentralize evaluation to the maximum possible extent 22
    Recognize that evaluation is not for amateurs 23
    Focus not just on enhancing collaboration and teamwork
        but also on "organizational motivation" 24

Conclusion 26

References 28

Appendix 31

Faculty members — and the departments they inhabit — are being subjected to more evaluation today than ever before. There are significant increases not only in the sheer amount of evaluation, but in the *sources* of evaluation. In addition to the now-standard methods of program review and regional accreditation, more recent mandates include "outcomes assessment," specialized and professional accreditation, and performance budgeting, to name a few. But what is the cumulative impact of all these on faculty work? Are faculty work lives changing? If so, in useful and constructive ways? Or is evaluation instead making faculty work more onerous and bureaucratic?

In this report we assess the ways in which academic departments in U.S. colleges and universities are evaluated, and we make several recommendations for improved practice.

This work continues an earlier line of inquiry, also published by the American Association for Higher Education (AAHE), as *The Collaborative Department: How Five Campuses Are Inching Toward Cultures of Collective Responsibility* (Wergin, 1994). That publication analyzed how five institutions were working to rally their faculty around a shorter and sharper list of goals, especially at the academic department level, and then negotiating with the departments how they would be held collectively accountable. The study suggested that even institutions that had made significant progress on the first task still had found it difficult to get very far on the second. In other words, focusing the mission is one thing, but developing workable unit evaluations is another. The challenges, as that report noted, are considerable:

> *The ideal approach would be to evaluate departments and other academic units in ways that are not too costly or time-consuming, that respect the diversity of disciplinary missions and cultures, and that promote departmental self-reflection, all while rewarding collective accomplishments appropriate to larger school and institutional missions. (13)*

But if the challenges are considerable, so are the stakes. Institutions of higher education and their faculties face enormous pressures. Public expectations of higher education have increased while public confidence has declined. It would appear — at least superficially — that many colleges and universities have "permitted an erosion of the culture of professional accountability by which [they] have traditionally assured

In this report we assess the ways in which academic departments in U.S. colleges and universities are evaluated, and we make several recommendations for improved practice.

the quality and standards of their academic programs and degrees" (Dill, 1999: 9). Skepticism has taken the form of new demands for accountability and support for alternative educational systems that promise a higher educational return for the dollar, including new proprietary institutions such as the University of Phoenix.

Faculty also face changing expectations. On the one hand, faculty face pressures from their institutions (and their colleagues) to increase their scholarly productivity, thereby raising institutional prestige and research income; on the other hand, they hear about how they need to pay more attention to all of the *other* things they do: to become more proficient with information technology, to revamp their pedagogy to reach an increasingly nontraditional student population, to become better university "citizens," to become more engaged with community and professional service, and so on. In short, "change" has often meant "do more."

Colleges and universities have responded by engaging in various "restructuring" activities, most of which assume that large-scale institutional change will sooner or later trickle down to departments[1] and affect faculty work. Some institutions have seen real change from these approaches (e.g., Eckel, Hill, and Green, 1998); but other institutions have not (cf., Larson, 1997), and in these cases "departmental culture" is usually fingered as the culprit. In a widely cited study, William Massy and his colleagues (1994) described patterns of "hollowed collegiality" within academic departments, characterized by faculty isolation, fragmented communication, and a reluctance to engage in the kind of truly collaborative work required to develop and maintain a coherent curriculum. Massy's findings ring true; but given the pressures for scholarly productivity, even in smaller institutions, it is not surprising that faculty members should act this way. Faculty typically are rewarded according to standards of quality dictated by their disciplines, not by standards specific to their institutions or departments (Fairweather, 1996). Since most faculty work alone — and are rewarded for working alone — there is little faculty investment in activities that require collective action, such as responding to institutional mandates for "accountability" or "assessment." Quite simply, many faculty members see little relationship between these mandates and the work they do or how they are rewarded for doing it. Faculty members do not necessarily reject the ideology behind reform; they simply do not see it as relevant to what they do and how they are rewarded.

> **Something has to give. Recent research provides some disturbing evidence of what happens when institutions and their faculties find themselves pulled in multiple and often conflicting directions.**

Something has to give. Recent research provides some disturbing evidence of what happens when institutions and their faculties find themselves pulled in multiple and often conflicting directions. One consequence is greater stress, especially for junior, tenure-eligible faculty, who worry about being able to "do it all" and to do it all equally well (Menges et al., 1999). What is often neglected, or "satisficed," is attention to teaching: Students report spending less time on learning activities yet they receive higher grades (Kuh, 1999). Faculty report becoming increasingly "disengaged" from their teaching and investing more of their time instead on research (Zusman, 1999), and college curricula have become fragmented and lack coherence (Gaff et al., 1997). Faculty stress is especially acute in universities with large numbers of academically underprepared students (Pitts, White, and Harrison, 1999).

The premise for the study reported here is that just as colleges and universities need to focus their missions and sharpen their priorities, so do faculty members. Faculty plates are already full, and adding new responsibilities without restructuring the work itself will only lead to greater stress, especially as long as evaluation and rewards are based on a "one size fits all" approach, which, in Gene Rice's words, leads to a "culture of competitive advantage."

Instead, what is needed is a different kind of culture, one in which faculty members are able to focus their efforts on activities that best draw upon their own skills, talents, interests, and experience, and which allows them to negotiate with their colleagues how they might best use these strengths to contribute to the work of the department. Thus, some faculty members might put relatively more effort into research, others into teaching, still others into institutional and professional service; and these areas of emphasis could shift throughout the course of a career.

Restructuring an institution to a new culture will be possible only when institutions shift the unit of analysis from the individual to the academic department; when the work of the department is evaluated as a whole, rather than simply as the aggregate of individual faculty accomplishments; and when faculty are evaluated according to their differential contributions to the group. As long as institutions respond to pressures for accountability with various exercises in strategic planning and creative mission building without also paying attention to change in how *departments* are evaluated and rewarded, they can expect only limited success.

OUR PURPOSE

In this paper we present and discuss the results of our survey on the evaluation of academic departments. Our original purpose was straightforward: to search for evaluation policies and practices that encourage constructive change in departments and a stronger culture of collective responsibility. We wanted to see (1) how these models worked, (2) what seemed most critical to their success, and (3) how key ideas might be applied to other settings.

But as the study progressed, our purpose shifted from a search for "models" to something slightly different: to identify elements of effective evaluation practice, and to put them together in a way that might provide harried administrators and faculty with a useful framework, or at least a visible point of reference.

After a brief methods section, we describe current practices, then abstract from these to describe key components of effective departmental evaluation. We end with several specific recommendations.

Methods and Procedures

We began this project in August 1998 by first reviewing the literature, both published and fugitive, including conference proceedings; posting messages on such listservs as the Association for the Study of Higher Education (ASHE) and the American Educational Research Association (AERA); arranging, through AAHE, for a mass mailing to all campus provosts; and calling upon personal networks of informants. We deliberately cast a wide net. The letter to provosts, for example, said,

> [We are] looking for exemplary models, tools, and processes for evaluation of academic departments <u>as units.</u> [We] intend to profile "best practices" and publicize good ideas — and hence to help the [Pew Charitable Trusts] identify future opportunities for wise investment. If your institution is engaging in innovative work on departmental or program review, [we] want to hear from you.

These efforts netted information on about 130 institutions across the Carnegie categories (see Table 1 in the Appendix). For some, the information we have is sparse: letters, email messages, or brief notes from telephone conversations. Other institutions provided more extensive guidelines and reports. As we combed through these data, we decided to analyze institutional practices in departmental assessment at three levels of intensity: (1) simply noting current practice; (2) writing a short profile based on campus documents and telephone interviews; and (3) undertaking more in-depth case studies with site visits. Selection of institutions for the last category was based upon complexity of mission (no baccalaureate or two-year institutions), distinctiveness of method, comprehensiveness of approach, and, in a couple of instances, hunches that a personal visit would be worthwhile.

We visited eight institutions: Georgia State University, Indiana University of Pennsylvania, Indiana University Purdue University Indianapolis, Northwestern University, St. Mary's University (TX), Southeast Missouri State University, the University of Arizona, and the University of Southern California.

Data-collection protocols varied with each visit and were determined by the nature of the idea or process under study. In most cases, we interviewed the provost or vice president for academic affairs, other members of the central academic administration, selected deans and chairs, and key faculty leaders. Visits lasted an average of one and a half days. We shared draft cases with institutional informants, and we incorporated corrections of fact — and sometimes inference — into our final drafts.

Campus Evaluation Practices

We were struck by the sheer amount of evaluation going on in academic departments. The collective work of faculty is evaluated in as many as five different ways, and some campuses employ all five. The problem is that often these methods are disconnected from one another.

Program review

Models for internal "program reviews" have been around for at least 15 years, and are now in place in most institutions. All but a handful of the institutions in our database employ formal program review in some form. The review either is cyclical (e.g., every five to seven years) or is triggered by financial or enrollment concerns. Typically, the department evaluates its strengths and weaknesses through a self-study and presents a plan for improvement, an external review panel visits the campus and writes a report, and a "program review committee" monitors the process.

The credibility of program reviews has suffered over the years for two reasons. First, even though program reviews are usually billed as "formative," their impacts on departments are generally modest (Mets, 1998). A second and related problem is that most program reviews are one-shot affairs, not integrated into the life of the institution. The process often unfolds in a way that encourages participants to get through it with a minimum of aggravation. The whole thing becomes tedious, time consuming, and often of little consequence. Because the focus is backward (on what has already happened) rather than forward (on what is possible), the review becomes a ritual. The opportunity for critical reflection — a chance to put the academic values of systematic inquiry to use — is lost in the desire to get the thing done.

We did find several exceptions to this pattern, however:

▶ Northwestern University is a prime example of an institution where program review is taken seriously: It is set in a culture that not only values collaboration across disciplinary lines but also places a high premium on program quality. The process at Northwestern University was designed and initiated by faculty members themselves; and while a substantial infrastructure has been built to administer program review, it is clearly there to serve the faculty.

▶ Another example of successful program review is Georgia State University, where reviews are guided by the institution's strategic goals and result in action plans with direct budgetary consequences.

▶ The University of Scranton has adopted "focused program review," an idea borrowed from Middle States Association guidelines. Instead of undergoing the standard comprehensive review, the department may opt, with the approval of the dean, to concentrate on a shorter list of questions of the department's own choosing. Reports from the institution are highly encouraging, suggesting that when departments are given the flexibility, they will ask themselves the difficult questions.

Outcomes assessment

Assessment has also become a common fixture in universities, but somewhat more recently, dating back to the late 1980s. The principal drivers for institutional assessment programs have been mostly external — various state agencies and legislatures and regional and professional accreditation associations. They have shifted the focus of assessment from "inputs" (such as campus resources) to documented student learning. Unlike program review, which focuses on the academic department, institutional assessment programs cut across the educational mission at various levels: the departmental major, general education, the baccalaureate degree. Outcomes assessment has met with mixed success in most institutions. As with program review, it seems that more attention is given to the mechanics associated with collecting and reporting data, and less to determining what kinds of data should be collected and how they can be used to improve student learning. In only a few institutions does the trajectory of assessment seem to cross that of program review; in these institutions, St. Mary's University, for example, outcomes assessment has supplanted program review by focusing assessment at the departmental level.

It seems that more attention is given to the mechanics associated with collecting and reporting data, and less to determining what kinds of data should be collected and how they can be used to improve student learning.

The two methods of evaluation do, however, share a rather dubious distinction: Faculty see the questions driving most assessment efforts as "theirs," not as "ours." The review is on someone else's agenda — higher administration, governing board, professional or disciplinary society. Most faculty accept the necessity of program review and outcomes assessment, but don't generally see these as processes that will affect their own professional practice, at least not in a positive way. Further, at most institutions, outcomes assessment data are not tied directly to the evaluation of departments as units. But as with program review, our survey turned up some notable exceptions:

▶ St. Mary's University not only puts assessment at the center of institutional priorities, but plans are mainly department based. While the administration makes it clear that assessment results will be important determinants of resource allocation at the school and departmental levels, individual units are encouraged to develop assessment plans that inform internal curricular decisions. Further, each department at St. Mary's identifies a faculty member to coordinate assessment and to help colleagues interpret the data.

▶ Worcester Polytechnic Institute has for the past 25 years required students to take three capstone courses — including one in the humanities — that require an integrative project. Student products not only are used to certify student competence but also serve collectively as the basis of annual departmental self-evaluations of teaching effectiveness.

▶ Ohio University, a research institution, also has a successful history of outcomes assessment at the departmental level. It has used "department-based assessment" since 1995; each year departmental faculty are asked to prepare a brief report focusing on evidence of completion of student learning objectives, both for majors and for other students taking their courses. Departmental reports are forwarded to the dean for review, and then on to the provost. An issue at Ohio is a tendency on the part of faculty to view assessment as top-down; as one informant noted, perhaps the best way to shift the focus to one of program improvement is to involve faculty members closely in developing a new process.

▶ At Baruch College, part of the City University of New York (CUNY) system, this problem has been met head-on with a "faculty-centered approach" to departmental review. Here — as with the other institutions mentioned — annual reviews are focused on learning outcomes, but departments are encouraged to be creative within general college and school guidelines.

Specialized accreditation

William Dill and others have written extensively about the limitations of specialized accreditation: What began as a mechanism for quality control in medical education has "metastasized" into nearly 100 specialized accrediting bodies, each holding local programs to standards that often ignore an institution's distinctive mission and goals (Dill, 1998). However, increasing numbers of specialized and professional accreditation agencies have rewritten their standards to focus on how well a program meets its learning goals *in ways consistent with institutional mission,* rather than on rigid, nationally normed standards.

The most striking of these are the guidelines proposed by the Accreditation Board for Engineering and Technology (ABET) and the AACSB–The International Association for Management Education. ABET, for example, has developed Engineering Criteria 2000, an approach that purports to increase the flexibility of accreditation criteria by focusing on standards of three general types: the degree to which the school practices "continuous quality improvement"; the degree to which students have the knowledge required for *entry* into the engineering profession; and the degree to which the school provides support *adequate for the program's objectives* (emphasis added). In this way, said Kate Aberle, associate executive director for ABET,

Several things happen. First, institutions and programs define their mission and objectives to meet the needs of their constituents, and thus enable program differentiation. Second, our emphasis on outcomes extends to basic preparation for professional practice. And third, we leave it up to the programs to demonstrate how these criteria and their educational objectives are being met." (personal communication, September 1998)

Other accrediting bodies now looking to similar, school-based criteria include the American Dental Association, the American Physical Therapy Association, the American Psychological Association, the American Council on Pharmaceutical Education, the National League for Nursing, and the American Occupational Therapy Association.

Financial accounting initiatives

Several universities have developed an accounting procedure called "activity-based costing" (ABC), which has been adapted from the business community. The principle underlying this method is "subsidiarity," or the idea that decisions about allocating resources need to be made at the level responsible for implementing those decisions. Two higher education models that employ modified techniques of ABC are the Stanford Cost Model (or "contribution margin analysis") and responsibility-centered management (RCM).

Contribution margin analysis subtracts costs from revenues for each school or other standard "cost unit." That figure represents the funds available to support the infrastructure of that unit (the "contribution margin"). A spreadsheet is then used to determine each unit's ratio of revenue to infrastructure cost. Since Stanford University operates on a central budget, the Stanford Cost Model has not been used for allocation decisions. It was designed instead to be one part of a programmatic review that would include such other factors as contributions to teaching, research productivity, national quality rankings, and so on. Nevertheless, the model has been used at Stanford University to help justify the reorganization of several departments.

Responsibility-centered management picks up where contribution margin analysis leaves off, by decentralizing fiscal responsibility and authority and pushing decision making to the school or department level. RCM also makes units responsible for generating income and managing expenses, and allows savings to be carried forward.

In theory, the key advantages of RCM are that (1) units develop increased awareness and accountability, (2) they gain flexibility and control over how funds are used, and thus (3) they are more motivated to improve program quality. Our sense, based on our review of RCM at the University of Southern California and Indiana University Purdue University Indianapolis, is that only the first two steps are achieved. That is, units do in fact become more fiscally responsible, and they do put their flexibility to creative use. We did not, however, see much evidence of greater attention to program quality under RCM, unless "quality" is defined as maximizing profit or minimizing loss. On the other hand, a common complaint about RCM — that it "balkanizes" academic units and thus reduces incentives for cooperation — seems overstated.

Internal quality assurance

Each of the above forms of unit evaluation is essentially "top-down" or "outside-in": that is, the stimulus is external to the department, and the emphasis is on account-ability to external constituencies. But unit evaluation focused solely on accountability is incomplete. Accepting the need to be "accountable" is one thing; developing a more internalized sense of *responsibility* for quality is another. Research on personal motiva-tion has shown that while external incentives may be important to gain our attention, *internal* motivation is what sustains us day-by-day (cf., Csikszentmihalyi, 1997).

While this promotion of CQI is still in the formative stages, it is an example of how institutions might truly restructure faculty work in ways that promote collaboration and collective responsibility.

Faculty members thrive to the extent that they gain intrinsic satisfaction from the work they do. But how are faculty to feel connected to an intellectual community in an increasingly privatized world? How, more particularly, might departmental faculty develop a sense of collective re-sponsibility for their work, a sense that their individual ef-fectiveness is inseparable from the effectiveness of the group?

Our survey turned up several examples of institu-tions that promote "continuous quality improvement" (CQI) at the departmental level; but few seem able to make the idea work. One moderately positive example is Indiana University of Pennsylvania's Reflective Practice Project. At IUP, departmental teaching circles have evolved into deeper departmental conversations about expectations for stu-dents, how these expectations translate into performance indicators, and how these indicators in turn relate to institutional measures. Seattle Pacific University is exploring ways of linking a series of institution-wide initiatives with "departmental development plans," which in turn are linked to individual faculty workplans. While this promotion of CQI is still in the formative stages, it is an exam-ple of how institutions might truly restructure faculty work in ways that promote col-laboration and collective responsibility. Finally, Northwest Missouri is one of the few institutions that has focused its discussions about "quality" at the level of the aca-demic department. In the words of provost Tim Gilmour,

> *We learned that we have to talk with each department individually: "How do we work together to find out what we need to know to get better? . . . We can't tell you what the best measures are — but there has to be a design and there have to*

be measures that tell you and us how well you're doing." (personal communication, June 1999)

But these cases are exceptional. In general, campus practices of quality assurance at the departmental level often suffer from two debilitating problems: lack of relevance and little coordination.

First, most departments and most faculty do not see the relevance of such practices to the work they do. The notion of "continuous quality improvement" has not taken hold. Faculty are already so busy with research and teaching that the idea of using evaluation for formative purposes is lost. Further, faculty view institutional measures of "quality" as off the mark, as not congruent with what their own definitions of quality might be. Consequently, program review and outcomes assessment exercises often have only marginal impact.

By contrast, successful campuses have a common theme: Faculty and departments have a strong influence on the purposes, processes, and methods of evaluation and on the evaluation questions asked. From this we infer that at the institutional level, demands for unit accountability should focus less on accountability for achieving certain predetermined results and more on how well units conduct evaluations for themselves and use the data these evaluations generate. This notion is similar to David Dill's ideas about "academic audit" (1999) and William Massy's ideas about "quality-process review" (1997): Rather than attempting to evaluate quality itself, the focus instead is on processes believed to *produce* quality. These ideas have sprung mostly from work in Western Europe (particularly the United Kingdom, Denmark, and the Netherlands) and Hong Kong, and they are directed mostly to the assessment of entire institutions; of those countries, only Denmark has a tradition of using the audit as a means of evaluating individual academic units (Thune, 1999).[2] Audits have yet to emerge as a viable alternative model in the United States at any level.

Second, there is little coordination at most institutions (except perhaps for scheduling) among assessment, program review, and external accreditation. It is ironic that the premium placed on administrative efficiency has not yet extended to activities that are presumed to make the institution more efficient. We were unable to locate a single institution where these activities complemented and informed one another well, with the possible exception of IUPUI, where all reviews of professional programs are negotiated to add value to their accreditation processes. Ohio University, among others, is working on improving coordination.

One additional problem should be noted. Even institutions with effective, workable systems of program review, such as Northwestern University, show huge variations across departments and schools. Sometimes campus policies seem to make little difference; what does matter is effective unit leadership, at both the school and departmental levels. We address this issue next, as we lay out a preliminary framework describing the qualities of effective departmental assessment.

Components of Effective
Evaluation at the Departmental Level

What makes evaluation of academic departments "effective"? We would suggest that effective evaluation informs judgments of quality that then lead to improved departmental functioning. Two key points are embedded in this statement: that evaluation informs judgments, it does not dictate them; and that evaluation promotes constructive change.

Our research to date suggests that when defined in this way, effective departmental assessment depends on three key factors:

▶ the degree to which the *organizational and cultural setting* promotes a conducive atmosphere for evaluation;

▶ the credibility and fairness of *evaluation policies and practices;* and

▶ the validity and reliability of *evaluation standards, criteria, and measures.*

We describe each factor in turn below.

ORGANIZATIONAL AND CULTURAL SETTING

The most important first step to quality assurance is not finding the right instrument or technique, but rather building an institutional climate supportive of quality improvement. When Northwestern University provost Lawrence Dumas was asked how he would go about initiating program review in another institution, he said this: "First I'd take a measure of the institution and its vision for the future. Is there ambition for change? I would try to find ways of articulating a higher degree of aspiration; if there weren't a strong appetite for this then program review would be doomed to failure" (personal communication, January 1999).

Here are some elements of a "quality" institutional climate as suggested by the institutions we reviewed.

A leadership of engagement
This is admittedly an all-encompassing term, but it characterizes leaders who are able to frame issues clearly, put clear choices before the faculty, and be open to negotiation about what will inform these decisions. In short, these are leaders who are able to make a clear and compelling case for why change is in the interest of the school or department and what the consequences of inaction will be. Leaders who engaged the faculty in this way were able to avoid the sort of "compliance mentality" that has

plagued so many institutional efforts at program review and outcomes assessment in the past.

A good example of an engaged leader is the dean of arts and sciences at Georgia State University. Shortly after the dean took office, he embarked on a process to make faculty salaries more equitable. Rather than doing this on an individual basis, he engaged the chairs as a group in a series of discussions about faculty productivity, focusing on the evidence chairs used to rate faculty quality. Over a period of five years, the chairs "normalized" their behavior, and salaries were adjusted accordingly.

Of all the elements of organizational climate, a leadership of engagement looks to be the most important.

Engaged departments

Once the case is made and the issues are framed, the department must continue the conversation. The ritual associated with program review is overcome when the department asks fundamental questions about itself, such as, "What are we trying to do? Why are we trying to do it? Why are we doing it that way? How do we know it works?" The review then takes on a purpose: It creates a link to the academic work of the department. The exercise thus moves beyond the belief that program review is mandated by "them" and is for "them."

The ritual associated with program review is overcome when the department asks fundamental questions about itself, such as, "What are we trying to do? Why are we trying to do it? Why are we doing it that way? How do we know it works?"

We observed the usefulness of this approach in two departments at the University of Arizona. The departments fostered a sense of ownership in program review by using it as an opportunity to talk about mutual objectives and how they could use evaluative data to advance their goals. Both departments began the review process by questioning where they currently were, where they wanted to be, and what they needed to do to best position themselves. As one department chair stated after what he considered a positive review experience, "Most [faculty] saw program review as advancing goals we set for ourselves. We worked hard to make it positive. We talked about how to approach this." In another department at Arizona, the self-study portion of the program review generated creative dialogue centered on change. "By looking at the issues it raised, we were forced to reevaluate who we are and dialogue between groups. We started with the education mission. Academic program review was the vehicle for change."

Faculty members who accept responsibility and ownership for program review and view it as the impetus for dialogue, a chance to reflect upon the work of the department, and a vehicle for possible changes are crucial to meaningful reviews centered on quality improvement.

A culture of evidence

This element is closely connected to the first two. A culture of evidence refers to a spirit of reflection and continuous improvement based on data, an almost matter-of-fact acceptance of the need for evidence as a tool for decision making. Institutions with strong cultures of evidence have a tradition of program review that is taken seriously (such as Northwestern University or Georgia State University), or have a campus culture where student outcomes assessment strongly influences curricular decisions and is part of the reward structure (such as St. Mary's University or Worcester Polytechnic Institute). A culture of evidence is unrelated to the *amount* of evidence: We reviewed several institutions that collect a great deal of information from and about academic units — as noted previously, much of those data disconnected — but do not nurture "cultures of evidence."

Two characteristics seem to promote cultures of evidence most positively. First, share data openly: Embrace the view that if information is power, then the sharing of information is empowerment. Second, the departments themselves should collect and interpret the data. In this way institutions hold departments accountable, not necessarily for specific results, but for taking assessment seriously and making appropriate changes. The experience of St. Mary's University shows how powerful a culture of evidence can be when departments are forced to define indigenous criteria for quality and what real success with students means for these departments.

Share data openly. Embrace the view that if information is power, then the sharing of information is empowerment.

A culture of peer collaboration and peer review

Faculty require substantial contact with the intellectual community. Two possible avenues of contact are through peer collaboration and peer review. Peer review is a potentially powerful and positive force, but only if it comes from well-informed colleagues who share a stake in the outcome. A central finding of AAHE's Peer Review of Teaching Project was that peer *review* is an empty exercise without peer *collaboration*. Our research suggests that the same can be said about the evaluation of departments: Unit evaluation is an empty exercise without unit collaboration. Departmental faculty find it extremely difficult to negotiate common criteria and standards for evaluation unless a collaborative culture already exists, and this in turn depends on faculty understanding one another's work.

Among the institutions in our database, Indiana University of Pennsylvania has pursued departmental collaboration — first by establishing cross-disciplinary teaching circles, then gradually shifting the focus to departmental faculty and their common expectations for students.

A respect for differences

If departments are to be evaluated as units rather than as the aggregate of faculty accomplishments, then differentiated faculty roles are essential. Kansas State University's program of "individualization" encourages departments to abandon the "one size fits all" mentality and to determine instead how to maximize individual faculty talents and interests. The key to doing this, according to associate provost Ron Downey, is for the institution to recognize and counter "the fear of becoming second-class": the concern that faculty members who choose to do relatively more teaching will find themselves having lower status than those doing more research (personal communication, February 1999). Creating greater faculty role differentiation will mean that in most departments the focus of evaluation will shift from judging by standards external to the unit ("merit") to judging the extent to which the faculty member is contributing to the mission of the unit ("worth"). Curiously, not much attention has been given to how differentiation of roles affects pretenure faculty members. Even at Kansas State University, pretenure faculty members have to prove they can "do it all" first.

Evaluation with consequence

Evaluation has to have a tangible, visible impact on resource allocation decisions. This assertion seems self-evident, even banal; but we found that it is not quite so simple as that. It is not a matter of "the more consequential the better." The most effective examples of program review did not go too far — they were not *so* consequential that the process turned into a high-stakes political exercise, where units felt compelled to puff up their successes and hide their weaknesses. The trick — as Northwestern University seems to have learned to do so well — is to use evaluation to help inform institutional decision making without appearing to rule it.

EVALUATION POLICIES AND PRACTICES

As we have already implied, the less the evaluation of departments is controlled by central administration and the less it is couched in terms of a *product* (that is, a report or series of recommendations) rather than as a *process* that contributes to continuous improvement, the more credible and thus more effective the evaluation is likely to be. We infer that organizational best practices are those that give maximum flexibility to units to define for themselves the critical evaluation questions, identify the key stakeholders and sources of evidence, and determine the most appropriate analysis and interpretation procedures.

Effective policies and practices as suggested by the institutions we studied have three important elements.

A clear purpose that fits the culture and mission of the institution

A "program review council" may work well at Northwestern University, which has a history of interschool cooperation, but may not at other schools lacking that tradition. Effective policies have clear purposes, and spell out the need for information. A clear understanding exists of how the results will inform resource allocation decisions, and what other factors will inform those decisions. Further, institutional policies regarding departmental assessment are integrated: departmental responsibilities for program review, outcomes assessment, and specialized accreditation are clearly spelled out so that the activities are complementary and redundancy is kept to a minimum.

"Spirit of inquiry" by the central administration

A department or other unit fosters a "spirit of inquiry" (Preskill and Torres, forthcoming) when it encourages its members to question assumptions, uncover problems without fear of punishment, and create new meanings and understandings. The focus of assessment is on current issues or problems, rather than on standard questions suggested by formal guidelines. The unit is encouraged to showcase its successes and to tell its story in its own way. Institutional performance indicators and/or external observers may be used, but as a means of raising issues of quality rather than answering them. Data are interpreted collectively, first by the departmental faculty, then with upper levels of administration. A high degree of faculty involvement occurs at all levels.

A department or other unit fosters a "spirit of inquiry" when it encourages its members to question assumptions, uncover problems without fear of punishment, and create new meanings and understandings.

Here are some examples of this principle in practice. At the University of Scranton (as noted earlier) departments may opt for "focused program reviews" in which departments address issues and concerns of their own choosing. At the University of Southern California, academic units are asked to develop their own "metrics of excellence," and the Rossier School of Education has responded by developing an "Academic Scorecard," which promises to be useful for internal decision making (see later discussion on page 20). At Baruch College, departments develop their own assessment plans within general College guidelines, and the College's institutional research office is charged with helping departments collect the data. At Belmont University, institutional measures of productivity are complemented by department-based assessments of student learning, defined in ways most meaningful to the department. And finally, at Southeast Missouri State University, procedures for awarding "departmental merit" are determined by each College Council, comprising two faculty members from each department, including the chair.

Tangible administrative follow-through

As we noted earlier, the evaluation must be consequential, but not rigid or formulaic. Unit assessment helps inform what is at heart a political process, and does so in a way that helps to open up what is often a "black box" of decision making. Rewards accrue to units that can show how they have used the assessment to solve problems and resolve issues. Action plans based on the evaluation are negotiated openly, with high levels of faculty involvement; and the administration communicates clearly the reasons for implementing — or not implementing — the action plans. Follow-through is often most effective when program evaluation is not carried out just every five to seven years but rather is done annually with periodic syntheses. Evaluation then becomes a standard process rather than a special event.

EVALUATION STANDARDS, CRITERIA, AND MEASURES

First, some definitions: *criteria* refers to the kinds of evidence collected as markers of quality; *standards* are the benchmarks against which the evidence is compared; and *measures* are the methods used to collect the evidence.

As Haworth and Conrad (1997) point out, one of the reasons why "quality" is such an elusive concept in higher education is the diversity of views held about what the criteria should be. They discuss four of these views: the "faculty view," which suggests that the principal criteria for evaluation should be the qualifications and productivity of the faculty; the "resources view," which stresses program size and financial and physical resources; the "student quality and effort view," which emphasizes student qualifications and achievements; and the "curriculum requirements view," which focuses on the rigor of the curriculum. Most common are various mixed models that include criteria from two or more of these approaches.

Haworth and Conrad note that these views of program quality all share similar problems: a heavy reliance on program "inputs," such as library resources; few empirical connections to student learning outcomes (and research that is further hampered by severe methodological limitations); an overreliance on quantitative indicators; and the general lack of attention to the views of such important stakeholders as students, alumni, and employers.

To those criticisms we would add another that may be most important of all: Current perspectives of program/departmental quality suffer from a lack of clarity and agreement about what the *standards* should be. We have found that with one important exception — namely, credible measures of student learning — institutions typically do not lack information that might lead to judgments about departmental quality; what they do lack is a shared understanding about how the information is to be interpreted. For example, what is the most appropriate standard for departmental research productivity: departmental goals negotiated earlier with the dean? last year's performance? the extent to which the scholarship fits within school priorities or the university's strategic plan? or how well the department stacks up against its "peer" departments in other institutions? Standards considered important or credible by one stakeholder group may not be considered important at all by another; thus, departmental quality will always be in the eye of the beholder. One definition of quality will not fit all (although ironically the one departmental attribute that is a consensus choice is the quality of student learning, the evidence that is the most difficult to collect).

Despite the diversity in institutional missions and policies regarding departmental assessment, the content of the evaluation — what is evaluated and how — does not vary much. We have combed through stacks of program review and assessment policies provided by our respondent institutions, and inventoried the criteria and measures (see Table 2 in the Appendix). We have sorted the data into criterion categories; these represent an amalgam of suggestions by the institutions we studied and by the assessment literature we reviewed. The list includes published criteria from research, doctoral, and master's institutions. No institution uses all or even most of these criteria, of course.

Despite the diversity in institutional missions and policies regarding departmental assessment, the content of the evaluation — what is evaluated and how — does not vary much.

The criteria are fairly evenly distributed across "inputs" (faculty qualifications, full-time employees), "processes" (curriculum quality, demands on students), and "outputs" (faculty publications, student learning). We had hypothesized that there would be a lack of attention given to student learning outcomes as part of departmental assessment, but instead found at least some of those criteria are generally used. When we looked carefully at the "process" criteria, however, we found relatively few that relate to how well a department promotes faculty and student learning, development, and growth.[3] If "continuous improvement" is a valued goal, it doesn't appear to be evaluated (and thus rewarded) very often.

In addition to the question of comprehensiveness is the issue of validity, or usefulness, of these criteria as evidence of departmental and program effectiveness. For example, how closely do the criteria displayed in these categories correspond to the "learning-centered" paradigms (Barr and Tagg, 1995) that have become so popular during the last decade? The answer to any question of validity depends on the extent to which the data fit the context: assessing "student quality" by computing acceptance ratios will be far more appropriate for a selective national university than for a comprehensive regional college. With that caveat in mind, it should be possible for individual institutions to examine carefully the evidence they use to assist with judgments about departmental effectiveness.

A framework for doing this is already available, in the form of *Program Evaluation Standards* (Joint Committee, 1994). While these standards were written generically to cover all forms of educational evaluation, most of them apply as well to the evaluation of postsecondary education as to other education programs. The standards are organized into four categories: *Utility* standards are intended to ensure that evaluation data will serve the information needs of the program's stakeholders; *feasibility* standards are intended to ensure that an evaluation will be realistic, prudent, diplomatic, and frugal; *propriety* standards are intended to ensure that the evaluation will be undertaken legally, ethically, and with "due regard" for those affected by its results; and *accuracy* standards are intended to ensure that the evaluation will convey "technically accurate information" about the program.

Accuracy standards address questions of data validity. One of the accuracy standards, paraphrased, says this: Information-gathering procedures should be developed in ways that will ensure that interpretations of data will be valid *for the intended use*. Criteria and measures are not inherently valid or invalid; rather validity "depends specifically on the questions being addressed, the procedure used, the conditions of the data collection, . . . and especially the interpretation of the results" (Joint Committee, 1994: 146). Guidelines for selecting the appropriate criteria include the following:

> ► Check evaluation criteria against the goals of the program; obtain judgments from stakeholders about the credibility of the criteria.[4]

> ► Specify reasons for selecting the criteria, and highlight the evidence that supports their use. Avoid selecting evidence just because it is quantifiable or readily available.

> ► Be especially careful when adopting new instruments, or instruments originally developed for another purpose. Do not rule them out, but point out that these instruments are exploratory, and must be interpreted with caution and within strictly defined contextual limits.

> ► Use multiple criteria and measures to accomplish a valid assessment, but do so in as nondisruptive and parsimonious a manner as possible.

> ► Assess the comprehensiveness of the information *as a set*, relative to the information needed to answer the set of evaluation questions.

Few guidelines for program review address questions of data validity, either in the directions for the departmental self-study or in the guidelines for external reviewers. This is an egregious omission, in our view. While it is true that there has been little empirical validation of most of the criteria used to assess program and departmental quality, there is no reason why the above five guidelines could not be followed. If they were, then some serious questions would be raised about the validity of at least some of the criteria that are currently recommended or required. Here is an example: At one flagship university, the assessment of "quality of instruction" includes these criteria: number of full-time faculty (undergraduate and graduate), total students per full-time faculty (undergraduate, master's, and doctoral), and degrees awarded per faculty (baccalaureate, master's, and doctorate). How, one might ask, do these indices qualify as markers of instructional quality? What do they have to do with the quality of student learning? Such criteria speak more to a department's *productivity* than to the quality of the instruction it provides.

A more positive example is what the Rossier School of Education did with the provost's "metrics of excellence" initiative at the University of Southern California. For the past five years, the provost's office has asked each school to identify quantitative measures of excellence most appropriate for the school's discipline(s) and to provide these data in advance of annual budget and planning meetings. Rossier School administrators viewed these annual reports to the provost as "laundry lists" that had little coherence and limited usefulness internally to substantive decisions about programs and resources. Rather than resign themselves to compliance, the School administration charged a faculty committee with designing a set of metrics that also would be useful internally, and this committee came up with the "Academic Scorecard," a four-part model adapted from the business world (O'Neil et al., 1999). Short lists of goals and measures were identified around each of four questions: "How do we look to central administrators? How do stakeholders see us? What must we excel at? How can we continue to improve?"

Few guidelines for program review address questions of data validity, either in the directions for the departmental self-study or in the guidelines for external reviewers. This is an egregious omission.

Key to the success of the Academic Scorecard, still under development, has been its explicit attention to (1) connecting performance criteria with goals and values of the School; (2) keeping the criteria simple and meaningful; and (3) selecting only those indicators that would facilitate improvement internally while, at the same time, making comparisons possible both within and outside the university. Notable about the School's work, in short, has been the attention the School has given to the quality and usefulness of the criteria *themselves*, thus increasing the chances for creating a culture of evidence and a climate of continuous quality improvement.

Recommendations for Evaluation Practice

Here we extrapolate from our findings and offer a few specific recommendations — ideas that, if followed, could aid in creating a more "self-regarding" institution, stronger and more widely accepted methods for evaluating departments as collectives, and eventually greater flexibility for departmental faculty.

These recommendations are not applicable to all settings. As we first began analyzing our reams of data, blanket recommendations seemed unattainable. Campus policies and methods of assessment seemed to blend together, and what most distinguished "effective" from "ineffective" assessment was the quality of leadership at the campus, school, and departmental levels. But as we dug more deeply into the findings, we became more comfortable in being specific about broad recommendations. We have kept the list short.

As we first began analyzing our reams of data, blanket recommendations seemed unattainable.... But as we dug more deeply into the findings, we became more comfortable in being specific about broad recommendations.

Be proactive in discussions of "quality"

We have observed already that little attention in our respondent institutions has been given to discussions of what "quality" means. Too many conversations about assessment proceed from the assumption of shared definitions of quality. To further complicate matters, traditional academic views of quality — disparate as they are — have been widely replaced by another, "marketplace" view that holds that quality is whatever we do that makes our "customers" happy. But as one of us has noted elsewhere (Wergin, 1998), too much responsiveness to the marketplace may itself be socially irresponsible. Being responsible means working for the common good; defining the common good, and thus defining what "quality" means, is thus a matter of negotiating interests. The criteria and standards used to define a "quality program" are multidimensional, and will vary according to who the stakeholders are.

At most institutions we reviewed, the assumption seems to be that determining quality is mostly a problem of data collection: that finding the right instrument or set of indicators will solve the evaluation problem. In the search for tools, the standards by which judgments of worth are made are largely ignored. We found the criteria and sources of evidence potentially useful for departmental evaluation to be plentiful. As for models to weigh the evidence, with explicit attention to stakeholder needs, we found only one: the Academic Scorecard now under development by the Rossier School of Education at the University of Southern California.

The message is plain. Any campus wishing to develop sounder and more useful evaluation of academic programs must address the multidimensional meanings of "quality." Departmental faculty will be more likely to take seriously an evaluation that uses criteria chosen for credibility, not just for convenience or accessibility of the evidence. We therefore recommend that any institution establishing or revising guidelines for program review and assessment subject potential assessment evidence to the criteria listed in Table 2 (see Appendix).

Decentralize evaluation to the maximum possible extent

The "maximum possible extent" is the point at which the evaluation strikes a meaningful balance between the objectives of the department and the appropriate needs of the institution.[5] A good way to encourage discussions of quality is to begin them at the level where they can be most specific and tangible; namely, in the academic programs themselves. One way for departments to reaffirm their commitment to academic quality is for them to embrace not just a set of mission and goal statements but a well-articulated set of principles that reflect quality attributes to which the department members aspire, and for which they are willing to be held mutually responsible.

A point of departure for this could be Haworth and Conrad's (1997) "engagement" theory of academic program quality. The authors' work was based on interviews with faculty members in forty-seven graduate programs distributed across eleven different disciplines. The authors anchor their perspective of quality on student learning, defining high-quality programs as those that "provide enriching learning experiences that positively affect students' growth and development" (27). An inductive analysis of their interview data revealed five clusters of associated program attributes: "diverse and engaged participants, participatory cultures, interactive teaching and learning, connected program requirements, and adequate resources" (1997: 28). Note that all five of these clusters reflect what the department has or what it does, not on learning outcomes themselves. In other words, these attributes are markers of what is presumed to be quality teaching and learning, just as Massy's (1997) notion of "quality-process reviews" assumes that "good people working with sufficient resources and according to good processes will produce good results" (253). Massy's model has been developed and implemented abroad; it and other forms of academic audit are virtually unknown in this country as a way of assessing *departmental* quality.

Given our sense of the barriers to effective departmental assessment, especially the limited utility of external performance indicators, we conclude that modified forms of quality-process review would have strong potential, particularly if linked to departmentally generated criteria and standards. For example, the dean of a college could develop guidelines specifying that departments are responsible for documenting (1) the processes by which their curricula are designed, reviewed, and improved; (2) the processes by which departmental faculty enhance instructional effectiveness; and

22   WERGIN AND SWINGEN

(3) how departments as a whole monitor student outcomes and link the outcomes to modifications in course design or delivery. Departments would then be free to develop specific methods of documentation, subject to negotiation with the dean. Such a process would honor the principles of good evaluation policy and practice listed earlier in this report.

Recognize that evaluation is not for amateurs

If evaluation is to be effective, institutional leaders must address the developmental needs of deans, chairs, and faculty. We do not mean to be pejorative about this, or to imply that program assessment should be turned over to a cadre of specialists. We only wish to suggest that using information well is a learned skill. Researcher Jennifer Haworth agrees: "Sometimes we assume that faculty know more than they do and we ask them to engage in institutional and departmental practices without providing them with a *foundational basis for effective practice*" (personal communication, March 1999). Faculty members trained as chemists, historians, or physical therapists usually receive little if any training in topics such as evaluating data quality and cross-examining evaluative evidence, even though these are crucial skills to bring to a review team.

> **Faculty members trained as chemists, historians, or physical therapists usually receive little if any training in topics such as evaluating data quality and cross-examining evaluative evidence, even though these are crucial skills to bring to a review team.**

Administrators often find themselves in the same boat. For example, the following issues arose in negotiations about departmental evaluation between the provost and a new dean at Indiana University of Pennsylvania. This case, like all others, of course, is singular: The university has a unionized culture with a history of suspicion between administration and faculty; but it also has undertaken a unique, grass-roots effort to define effectiveness at the departmental level. Preliminary concerns and issues were these:

▶ It is difficult to reward departmental performance when your operating budgets are frozen and salary increases are lock-step.

▶ Giving departments too much latitude in their own evaluation might result in complacency; but it is important also to recognize the power of intrinsic motivation in a department that works together more effectively.

▶ How should rewards be distributed at the unit level: to support needy departments at the expense of the productive ones, or vice versa?

▶ Any ultimate solution will require individual faculty work agreements, each different but which together will meet departmental and college goals. How to do that is a mystery.

While the above were stated within the context of a single college in a single university, most deans will recognize such problems as ones they have faced themselves. Any change effort must recognize the difficult, practical, "in the trenches" problems that deans and department chairs must face, and no model or set of procedures will provide an easy solution to those problems. Deans and chairs need opportunities to reflect on their practice, gain insights of their peers, adapt and "try on" new ideas, gain feedback from their constituencies, and make changes that have optimal risk. As Smith (1998) discovered in a two-year "futures project" with colleges and universities in California, concrete learning from active experimentation is much more powerful than is engaging in planning exercises that assume that progress is something linear and rational.[6]

Focus not just on enhancing collaboration and teamwork but also on "organizational motivation"

The problem that dogs many administrators is how to foster a department's internal commitment to quality and change.

Quality assurance happens within a department. It cannot be imposed by administrative directives, leadership efforts, or program review alone. Program review can help identify needs for change and quality improvement; and an effective, systematic program evaluation can inform judgments of quality. But improved departmental functioning requires commitment of the faculty as a collective. Only departmental faculty can define quality in the discipline and use evaluative information to determine whether they meet standards. The sustained effort and energy needed to work toward a high standard of quality can only come from the unified efforts of the faculty.

The problem that dogs many administrators — and one of the most common themes emerging from our site visits — is how to foster a department's internal commitment to quality and change. How can an institution reconcile its faculty members' personal goals (needs for income, security, academic freedom, and autonomy) with the collective goals of the department and the institution? We have written earlier in this report about the power of internal motivation in faculty life, and how some departments — even in schools with otherwise weak leadership — have become more unified and have begun to function as a team with a set of unified goals. How does this happen? How does the rhetoric of "continuous quality improvement" become part of the departmental fabric?

The answer will have more to do with culture than with structure, as Tierney (1999) points out — and departmental culture is not well understood. Simply encouraging collaboration is not likely to work; a deeper understanding of faculty preferences is needed. Barry Staw (1984) has adapted earlier writings on motivation in organizations for the academic environment. He notes that the interaction between "extrinsic" and "intrinsic" rewards is complex: that in settings where pay represents the only tangible feedback on performance, monetary rewards may be sought more for their symbolic than their economic value,[7] although external rewards become more salient when universities are faced with shrinking resources and faculty members find themselves competing with one another for those resources. An additional complication, according to Staw, is that university cultures, with their traditions of autonomy and self-governance, grant considerable latitude to faculty to set their own objectives and determine their own roles. Therefore it is important for the institution to set priorities and provide sufficient "time, resources, and social support" so that faculty "believe they can perform their roles effectively as well as perceive some benefit from their performance" (Staw, 1984: 69). Some recent research provides at least partial support for this point, indicating that faculty motivation to participate in educational reform depends on faculty role preferences and their expectations of what their involvement would yield (Serow, Brawner, and Demery, 1999).

If the unit of assessment is to shift from individual to collective achievement, however, then a different model of motivation is needed. Staw's persuasive suggestion is that "organizational motivation" — the likelihood that faculty members will "contribute to the collective product" rather than act strictly from self-interest — is a function of two interacting variables: the degree to which faculty members identify with their institution, and the perceived probability that their behavior will affect the institution in a positive way.[8] This suggests that rather than focusing *all* of their attention on "reward systems," university administrators would be well advised to nurture faculty members' affiliation with the institution, through socialization experiences, ceremonies, and other symbolic acts; by acknowledging individual faculty members whose work benefits the institution; and by removing existing disincentives to participation in institutional citizenship.

Conclusion

Smith (1998) concluded from the "futures project" that institutions are best able to accomplish real change if they have what she called "organizational capital" — that is, widely shared institutional values that lead to operational goals; trust and openness that enables discussions across departmental lines; faculty who are developed and valued as educators and contributors to the health of the institution; widespread awareness of the external context; opportunities for institutional members to understand, reflect on, and exchange information with others about their roles and those of their institution; and support for those willing to experiment and take risks.

While her findings were obtained under vastly different circumstances and for totally different purposes, they are remarkably similar to ours. Among the institutions we studied, the most successful with departmental and unit assessment were those institutions where administrators took the long view: where they took the time to develop a commitment to and an energy for change (to develop organizational capital, in other words), and then looked to evaluation to help move the change along.

The most successful with departmental and unit assessment were those institutions where administrators took the long view.

The way an institution sees itself is reflected in how it evaluates. Unless congruence exists between what an institution espouses and what it practices, the evaluation of its faculty members and the academic units they inhabit will be frustrating, ritualistic, and distrusted. In contrast, unit assessment that takes place in a climate supportive of quality improvement, that enhances organizational motivation by treating the department as a collective, that gives departments maximum flexibility to identify and answer their own evaluation questions, and that takes seriously issues of data quality and credibility will be both effective and growth-producing.

Notes

1. In this paper we define "departments" as the smallest units of an academic organization.

2. David Dill (personal communication, 1999) advises caution in considering European "audits" as potentially analogous to American "program reviews." As he points out, in the United Kingdom, Denmark, and the Netherlands, separate external agencies carry out "subject" reviews, which assume a more standard curriculum and more universal "academic standards" than are assumed to exist in this country.

3. We are indebted to Jennifer Haworth for this insight.

4. At IUPUI, community representatives are present as a matter of policy on program review committees and serve this function, at least in part.

5. Our thanks to Bob Barak for contributing this insight.

6. We are indebted to Dan Tompkins of Temple University for alerting us to this work.

7. We saw evidence of this in the Southeast Missouri case, where even small differences in "departmental merit" pay were taken very seriously by departmental faculty.

8. Bensimon and O'Neil (1998) have suggested that individuals consciously working for the benefit of group goals is itself a type of collaboration ("individual-organizational collaboration") that is at least of equal value to more traditional notions of "teamwork."

References

Barr, R.B., and J. Tagg. (November/December 1995). "From Teaching to Learning: A New Paradigm for Undergraduate Education." *Change* 27(6): 12-25.

Bensimon, E.M., and H.F. O'Neil. (1998). "Collaborative Effort to Measure Faculty Work." *Liberal Education* 84(4): 22-31.

Csikszentmihalyi, M. (1997). *Finding Flow: The Psychology of Engagement With Everyday Life*. New York, NY: Basic Books.

Dill, D. (June 1999). "Implementing Academic Audits: Lessons Learned in Europe and Asia." Unpublished manuscript prepared for the Academic Audit Seminar, Chapel Hill, NC.

Dill, W.R. (July/August 1998). "Specialized Accreditation: An Idea Whose Time Has Come? Or Gone?" *Change* 30(4): 18-25.

Eckel, P. (Winter 1998). "Thinking Differently About Academic Departments: The Academic Department as a Team." In *Teams and Teamwork in Institutional Research*, edited by S. Frost. New Directions for Institutional Research, no. 100. San Francisco, CA: Jossey-Bass.

——— , B. Hill, and M. Green. (1998). *On Change: En Route to Transformation*. Washington, DC: American Council on Education.

Fairweather, J. (1996). *Faculty Work and the Public Trust: Restoring the Value of Teaching and Public Service in American Academic Life*. Boston, MA: Allyn & Bacon.

Gaff, J.G., J.L. Ratcliff, and Associates. (1997). *Handbook of the Undergraduate Curriculum: A Comprehensive Guide to Purposes, Structures, Practices, and Change*. San Francisco, CA: Jossey-Bass.

Haworth, J.G., and C.F. Conrad. (1997). *Emblems of Quality in Higher Education: Developing and Sustaining High-Quality Programs*. Boston, MA: Allyn & Bacon.

Joint Committee on Standards for Educational Evaluation. (1994). *Program Evaluation Standards*. 2nd ed. London, England: Sage.

Kuh, G.D. (1999). "How Are We Doing? Tracking the Quality of the Undergraduate Experience, 1960s to the Present." *Review of Higher Education* 22(2): 99-119.

Larson, R.S. (1997). "Organizational Change From the 'Inside': A Study of University Outreach." Dissertation, Michigan State University.

Massy, W.F. (1997). "Teaching and Learning Quality Process Review: The Hong Kong Programme." *Quality in Higher Education* 3(3): 249-262.

———, A.K. Wilger, and C. Colbeck. (July/August 1994). "Overcoming 'Hollowed' Collegiality: Departmental Cultures and Teaching Quality." *Change* 26(4): 10-20.

Menges, R.J., and Associates. (1999). *Faculty in New Jobs: A Guide to Settling In, Becoming Established, and Building Institutional Support*. San Francisco, CA: Jossey-Bass.

Mets, L.A. (1998). "Implementation Strategies in a University Setting: Departmental Responses to Program Review Recommendations." Dissertation, University of Michigan.

O'Neil, H.F., E.M. Bensimon, M.A. Diamond, and M.R. Moore. (1999). "Academic Scorecard." Unpublished manuscript, University of Southern California.

Pitts, J.M., W.G. White Jr., and A.B. Harrison. (1999). "Student Academic Under-preparedness: Effects on Faculty." *Review of Higher Education* 22(4): 343-365.

Preskill, H., and R.T. Torres. (Forthcoming). "Evaluative Inquiry for Organizational Learning." In *Learning Around Organizations: Developments in Theory and Practice,* edited by M.E. Smith, L. Araujo, and J. Burgoyne. London, England: Sage.

Serow, R.C., C.E. Brawner, and J. Demery. (1999). "Instructional Reform at Research Universities: Studying Faculty Motivation." *Review of Higher Education* 22(4): 411-423.

Smith, V. (1998). "The Futures Project: A Two-Year Activity of 18 Independent Colleges and Universities in California." Final report to the James Irvine Foundation.

Staw, B.M. (1984). "Motivation Research Versus the Art of Faculty Management." In *College and University Organization: Insights From the Behavioral Sciences,* pp. 63-84, edited by J.L. Bess. New York, NY: New York University Press.

Thune, C. (June 1999). "European Developments in Academic Quality Assurance." Paper presented to The Academic Audit Seminar: Lessons Learned in Europe and Asia, Chapel Hill, NC.

Tierney, W.G. (1999). *Building the Responsive Campus: Creating High Performance Colleges and Universities*. London, England: Sage.

Wergin, J.F. (1994). *The Collaborative Department: How Five Campuses Are Inching Toward Cultures of Collective Responsibility.* Washington, DC: American Association for Higher Education.

———— . (June 1998). "Assessment of Programs and Units: Program Review and Specialized Accreditation." Paper presented at the AAHE Assessment Conference, Cincinnati, OH.

Zusman, A. "Issues Facing Higher Education in the Twenty-First Century." (1999). In *American Higher Education in the Twenty-First Century,* pp. 109-150, edited by P.G. Altbach, R.O. Berdahl, and P.J. Gumport. Baltimore, MD: Johns Hopkins.

Table 1.
Institutions Reviewed
(Grouped by Carnegie Classification)

Unless otherwise noted, all institutions employ traditional program review.
An asterisk (*) indicates information gathered electronically.

Institution	Notable Qualities
Research I	
Duke University (NC)	
Massachusetts Institute of Technology*	
Michigan State University	Attention to review of interdepartmental programs
Northwestern University (IL)	Well-established policies/procedures; extensive research base
Stanford University (CA)	"Margin/cost analysis"
Syracuse University (NY)*	Mission-driven evaluation
Texas A&M University	
University of Arizona	
University of Cincinnati-Main Campus	
University of Connecticut	
University of Florida	Quality/productivity benchmarks; performance-based budgeting
University of Kansas	
University of Nebraska, Lincoln	
University of Southern California	Well-established system of RCM; now reconsidering
University of Virginia	
University of Washington	
University of Wisconsin, Madison	Assessment of "program array"
Virginia Polytechnic Institute and State University*	

Research II	
Brigham Young University (UT)	
George Washington University (DC)	Links to strategic plans and resource allocation
Kansas State University	Policy for differentiated faculty roles ("Individualization")
Kent State University (OH)	Reviews connected to "abbreviated Responsibility Center Budgeting"
Lehigh University (PA)	European model of "visiting committees"
Northeastern University (MA)	Departmental goals/evaluation driven by strategic plan
Ohio University	Department-based assessment of student outcomes
University of Delaware	Block grants to colleges based on mission performance
University of Notre Dame (IN)	Links to strategic planning and outcomes assessment

Doctoral I	
Bowling Green State University (OH)*	
Fordham University (NY)	
Georgia State University	Linkages among methods, strong sense of mission, open negotiation of criteria/standards
Indiana University of Pennsylvania	Grass-roots definitions of program quality through "Reflective Practice"
State University of New York at Binghamton	
University of North Carolina, Greensboro	Focus on instructional quality

Doctoral II	
George Mason University (VA)	
Indiana University Purdue University Indianapolis	Responsibility-centered budgeting, economic analyses
Texas Christian University	"Consequential goal setting"
Worcester Polytechnic Institute (MA)	Student educational products as departmental assessment

Master's I	
Angelo State University (TX)	Academic master plan
Ashland University (OH)	Extensive guidelines; "white papers" as adjunct documents; assessment links
Boise State University (ID)	Links to accreditation; detailed criteria
California State University, Stanislaus	Detailed program criteria, links to strategic planning
City College of New York, Baruch College	"Faculty-centered" approach
City College of New York, Hunter College*	
College of New Jersey	Student-centered focus
Converse College (SC)	No formal program review: assessment data analyzed at department level
Gallaudet University (DC)	Annual unit reports tied to strategic objectives
Lesley College (MA)	Learning goals x evidence matrix
Marshall University (WV)*	Program review guidelines mandated by the state
Moorhead State (MN)	Biennial reports + six-year reviews, tied to budget
Our Lady of the Lake University (TX)	
Prairie View A&M University (TX)	Benchmarking of departments with peers in other institutions
Seattle Pacific University (WA)	Work toward creation of team-based departments
South Dakota State University	Extensive guidelines
Southeast Missouri State University	Departmental merit; departmental reports basis for linkages among methods
St. Francis College (PA)	Links to outcomes assessment
St. Mary's University (TX)	Outcomes assessment done in lieu of program review
University of Alaska, Anchorage*	Developing integrated model: program review, assessment, budgeting
University of Hartford (CT)	Includes income and expense analyses by department
University of Houston-Victoria (TX)	
University of North Carolina at Charlotte	Web-based links among strategic planning, assessment and annual reports
University of Portland (OR)*	Use of program review to make structural and curricular changes, review process emphasizes assessment
University of Scranton (PA)	Use of annual departmental reports; "focused program review"

Villanova University (PA)*	Detailed and precise measurement of finances and teaching loads are used in self-study
West Chester University of Pennsylvania	Links to resource allocation decisions

Master's II	
Belmont University (TN)	Annual departmental assessment, tied to strategic goals & budget
Drury College (MO)	
University of Wisconsin-Green Bay	Inclusion of "program development plan" with learning outcomes

Baccalaureate I	
Franklin College (IN)*	Connection to "student learning plans"
Georgetown College (KY)	Just beginning program review
Goucher College (MD)*	Formal follow-up process
Hartwick College (NY)*	Integration with other campus initiatives
Houghton College (NY)	
Smith College (MA)	

Baccalaureate II	
Allentown College of St. Francis de Sales (PA)	
Augustana College (SD)	"Inside-out" process
Berry College (GA)	Examples included
Campbellsville University (KY)	
Dordt College (IA)	Use of "course goals inventory"
Greensboro College (NC)	
Jarvis Christian College (TX)	Used the Malcolm Baldrige criteria to review a department last spring
Johnson C. Smith University (NC)	Review focuses on departmental productivity, faculty load, and program quality
Kentucky Wesleyan (KY)	Mission-based; conscious follow-through
King's College (PA)	Five-year formative process focusing on the future
Lawrence Technical University (MI)	
Lebanon Valley College (PA)	Departmental self-evaluation protocols
Martin University (IN)	Classroom assessment tied to program review

McPherson College (KS)	Triggered review; separation of program assessment (merit) from review (worth)
Merrimack College (MA)	"Program-based management"
Mount Vernon Nazarene (OH)	
Seton Hill College (PA)	
Shorter College (GA)*	
Western Baptist College (OR)	Desire to implement new process because of financial pressure

Associate's	
Hagerstown Junior College (MD)	Division chair workload model
Chabot College (CA)	Extensive criteria/measures
College of the Redwoods (CA)	
College of the Sequoias (CA)*	Annual departmental self-studies
Cuyahoga Community College (OH)	Review intensity triggered by indicators
Cuyamaca College (CA)	Outcomes-based accreditation standards
Delaware Technical and Community College	Statistical review of enrollment, retention, and graduation rates across 5 years by program
Floyd College (GA)	Only 2-year in GA system with program review
Fox Valley Technical College (WI)*	Annual review process for "health" indicators in addition to outside audit team
Greenville Technical College (SC)	Uses DACUM (Developing a Curriculum) model
Grossmont College (CA)	
Herkimer County Community College (NY)	
Hudson County Community College (NJ)	Links with institutional accreditation
Jefferson College (MO)	
Johnson County College (KS)	Extensive documentation; links to outcomes assessment
Lehigh Carbon Community College (PA)	Learning-competency based
McHenry County College (IL)*	SCANS instrument to measure liberal learning
Mesa Community College (AZ)	Combination of outcomes assessment in occupational programs and program review
Nassau Community College (NY)	"User-friendly" computerized model
Niagara County Community College (NY)	Extensive examples of assessment tools
Orange Coast College (CA)	
Polk Community College (FL)	Learning outcomes/ indicators for programs
Riverside Community College (CA)	Connection between program review and new program development

San Jacinto College (TX)	
Terra Community College (OH)	Link to Policy Governance (Board of Trustees); concise format: "What good? For what people? At what cost?"
Trident Technical College (SC)	Systematic use of Goal Attainment Scaling; extensive documentation
Volunteer State Community College (TN)	Cross-department program review, tied to student assessment
Western Wisconsin Technical College	Linked to Continuous Improvement Process

Art, Music, and Design	
Otis College of Art and Design (CA)	

Business	
Lynn University (FL)	Does assessment at unit level, which feeds into institution-wide assessment

Engineering	
Rose-Hulman Institute of Technology (IN)	Use of electronic student portfolios as basis for assessment of departments
Webb Institute (NY)	

Medical	
Baylor College of Medicine (TX)	Faculty-developed statistical "metrics" measuring quality across all missions
University of Colorado Health Sciences Center	

Religion and Theology	
Minnesota Bible College	
North Central University (MN)	Program "audits" with "end-sought" statements

Other Specialized	
U.S. Military Academy (NY)	Mission-driven evaluation

Table 2.
Evidence Used
for Departmental Assessment
(Research, Doctoral, and Master's Universities)

Criteria   Measures/Sources of Data

Faculty Qualifications	
Academic origins/credentials	Faculty vitae
National prominence	
Qualifications of adjuncts	
Potential for response to future needs/opportunities	
Congruence of faculty qualifications with dept. needs/goals	
Faculty development opportunities	

Faculty Productivity	
Research funding	
Faculty publications	Vitae, citation indices
Scholarly awards	
National standing (dept.)	NRC rankings
Teaching loads	
Student credit hours (SCH) taught	
Dispersion of faculty FTE	
Theses advised, chaired	
Students supervised	
Service contributions	
Academic outreach	
Collaboration with other units or programs	

Efficiency	
Trends in unit costs	Institutional/state averages
Faculty/student FTE	
Faculty/staff FTE	
SCH/faculty FTE	
Revenues/SCH	
Revenues/costs	
Operating budget/faculty FTE	
Research expenditures/faculty FTE	
State support/total budget	

Curriculum Quality	
Planning processes	
Quality control mechanisms	
Learning goals	Comparisons with "field" standards
Requirements for major or grad. degree	Comparisons with "benchmarks"
Congruence of course/curricular goals	Course/curricular matrices
Course coordination	Course sequence charts
Prerequisite patterns	
Balance between breadth and depth	
% courses denoted as "active learning"	
Uniformity across multiple course sections	
Availability of electives	
Advising procedures	
Role in gen. ed./service courses	
Adjunct usage	
Existence of student portfolios, competency exams, capstone courses	
Curricular revision procedures	

Pedagogical Quality	
Processes for evaluation of teaching, advising	Recognition by constituencies
Engagement in collaborative teaching	
Class size	
Pedagogical innovation	
Quality of syllabi	
Strategies for promoting active learning	

Procedures for setting academic standards	
Adoption of information technology	

Student Quality	
Entering GRE scores; SATs	
Recruitment strategies	
Acceptance ratio	
Support for graduate students ($)	

Student Productivity	
Demographic diversity	
Enrollment patterns	Comparisons to inst./state figures
Number of majors	
Number of transfers in	
Demands on students	
Student effort	College Student Experiences Questionnaire
Retention/graduation rates	
Degrees awarded	
Time to degree	
Student involvement in dept. activities	

Learning Outcomes	
Processes for evaluation of learning	
Student development	Student journals, portfolios
Student satisfaction	HEDS Consortium Senior Survey, exit interviews
Grade distributions	
Mastery of generic skills	Academic Profile
Student achievements	Accomplishment of objectives in major
Performance in capstone courses	
Student placement	Surveys of graduates
Employer satisfaction	Surveys of employers
Alumni satisfaction	Alumni surveys
Performance on licensing/certification exams, standardized tests	GRE, etc. scores
% graduates entering graduate school	

Adequacy of Resources	
Laboratory/computer facilities	
Faculty offices	
Classrooms	
Support staff	
Enrollment capacity	

Contribution to Institutional Mission/Priorities	
Departmental mission/vision	
Departmental distinctiveness	"Benchmark" departments
Centrality to institution	
Availability of program elsewhere	
Relationship to other programs	
Contribution to economic development, other social benefits	
Service to nonmajors, continuing education	
Fit with strategic plan	
Student demand	
Employer demand	Occupational demand projections

Other	
Progress since last review	
Comparative advantages	
Unique future opportunities	
Status re: accreditation requirements	